First edition for the United States and Canada © copyright 2001 by Barron's Educational Series, Inc.

First edition for Great Britain published 2000 by Hodder Wayland,
an imprint of Hodder Children's Books

Text © Pat Thomas 2000
Illustrations © Lesley Harker 2000

All inquiries should be addressed to:
Barron's Educational Series, Inc.
250 Wireless Boulevard
Hauppauge, NY 11788
http://www.barronseduc.com

Library of Congress Catalog Card No. 00-105772

International Standard Book No. 0-7641-1763-7

Printed and bound in Italy

9 8 7 6 5 4 3 2 1

My Friends and Me

A FIRST LOOK AT FRIENDSHIP

PAT THOMAS
ILLUSTRATED BY LESLEY HARKER

BARRON'S

You probably know lots
of other children.

But only a few of them
are your friends.

Some people like to have lots of friends around them.

And other people like to have one or
two special friends to play with most
of the time.

A friend can be anyone or anything that you enjoy being with.

It can even be someone that no one else can see! This is a way to play by yourself.

A friend can be someone with whom you can laugh and be loud. Or someone you can play quietly with.

What about you?

Who are your friends? What sort of things do you do together?

Have you ever thought about what makes a good friend?

A friend is someone who you feel comfortable and safe with. It is someone who shares and who keeps promises.

A friend wants to understand how you feel –
and likes you just the way you are.

It is someone who encourages you to be yourself –
even if it means being different from others.

Occasionally you might think someone
is a friend – but someone
who is mean to you
is probably not
your friend.

But a true friend won't ask you to do things that get you into trouble with your parents or your teachers. Anyone who does this does not deserve your friendship.

Sometimes, without meaning to, you may say or do something that hurts your friend.

You may get jealous when he plays with someone else and tries to take your friendship away.

But friendship is often best when you can share it.
And with a good friend it's not so hard to say,
"I'm sorry," when you've done something hurtful.

What about you?

Do you ever fight with your friends?
What things do you fight about?

We all have times when
we think nobody likes us.
And it isn't always easy to
make friends,
especially if
you feel shy.

18

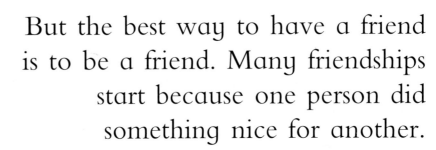

But the best way to have a friend is to be a friend. Many friendships start because one person did something nice for another.

There are lots of things in life that you don't have a choice about. You have to go to school, and brush your teeth, and eat your vegetables.

But you do have a choice about what people are your friends.

Every day you will meet lots of different people. You should always try to be kind and fair to everyone you meet.

But this does not mean that you have to be friends with everyone. You can know someone and get along with them without being a friend.

What about you?

Can you think of examples of people you know who are friends and not friends? What's the difference?

You also have a choice about how you behave with your friends. You can choose whether to be nice or mean, whether to argue or agree.

If you choose to do things like hitting, not sharing, or wanting everything your way, you may find it's a lot harder to make friends. Other people only want to be with you when you treat them well.

Having a friend and being a friend can make you feel good about yourself.

And when you feel good
about yourself, anything is possible.

HOW TO USE THIS BOOK

Friendship is one of the fundamental ways in which we begin to develop social skills such as empathy, sharing, how to appreciate the differences between people, how to express ourselves – in joy and in anger – and how to negotiate our needs in relation to the needs of others. Help your children make positive choices about their friends and about their behavior toward their friends by encouraging positive behavior.

Imaginary friends are not real friends, but they are very important. Children can try out lots of situations on imaginary friends and behave in ways that they couldn't with real friends. It can be hard, even frustrating, for adults to take such friends seriously, but it's a good idea to try. Allow the imaginary friend as much space in the family as you can. When your child has finished trying out this friendship, he or she will move on.

At some point your child is going to make friends with someone you don't like or who you feel is a bad influence. Childhood friendships are very complicated and intense and your disapproval may make the attraction more intense. Instead, try to reinforce your child's more positive relationships. Also ask yourself what your child needs from this particular person at this particular time. Children's friendships go through many changes during these early years. Chances are with positive reinforcement of healthier relationships the change will be for the better.

As society becomes more mobile, it is very common for a friendship to end because one friend moves away. Sometimes moving away is a natural ending to a friendship and other times it is not. If your child is grieving for the loss of a friend, help them to keep in touch by letter, or by e-mail, or, if feasible, by occasional visits, while gently encouraging new friendships.

Friendship can bring lots of pleasure, but it can also bring a lot of anguish as children move in and out of each other's lives and learn how to negotiate personal boundaries and needs. Try to support your child through these difficult times rather than isolate or protect them.

Although friendship is very important in our lives, most of our training is on the job. Issues about friendship are very common in school and the playground, and this is a good time to get children thinking about what it means to be a friend and which people in their lives are friends and which are not friends. A good class project is to produce a list of twelve ways you can be a good friend. When everyone is in agreement, you can make and decorate a poster to keep in the classroom. You can also use the list for homework, asking each child to provide examples from their own lives of how they have been a good friend.

GLOSSARY

Jealousy is a feeling you have about another person. When we get jealous we are worried that another person is taking someone else's friendship, love, and attention away from us. Talking to someone you trust about jealous feelings can be reassuring.

Friendship
When you first meet someone, friendship is usually just a nice feeling that you have about them. But when you have known someone a long time friendship will also be the way you act toward them. Thinking about your friends' feelings and treating them kindly are important ways to show friendship.

FURTHER READING

Friends by Elaine Scott (Atheneum, 2000)

How to Be a Friend by Laurie Krasny Brown and Marc Brown (Little, Brown, 1998)

Me First! Me First! by The Berenstains (Random House, 2000)

Two Girls Can by Keiko Narahashi (Simon & Schuster, 2000)

RESOURCES

The Parents Network
Contact the church of your faith and see what Sunday School programs they have on the topic of friendship for young children.

Contact your child's elementary school counselor and see what instructional materials are used to teach about friendship in the classroom.

9- 22-03: 9